The Best of Donna Magazine Store:

A

Catalog

Of

Donna Magazine Store

Products

The Best of Donna Magazine Store:

A

Catalog

Of

Donna Magazine Store

Products

By

Donna KAKONGE

@ Donna Kay Cindy KAKONGE

ISBN: 9798353253709

Printed in the United States

Cover Design

By

Donna Kay Cindy KAKONGE

Introduction

Currently Donna Magazine which was a magazine and blog is focused on being an affiliate marketing store, plus introduces classes right on the magazine's site that is powered by Wordpress.com.

It contains:

Advertorials Written About these Amazing Affiliate Partners: Adobe, ADSWAPPER, Amazon, Apple, AWIN, CLICKBANK,

Commission Factory, Commission Junction, ENCYL Digital, FINTEL Connect, Involve Asia, Jasper.ai, LINGODA, OFFERVAULT, OUTSCHOOL, PARTNERNIZE, Paysale.com, Pictory.ai, Rakuten, Sapling, SHAREASALE, SITEGROUND, SOVRN (VIGILINK), Synthesia.io, TextCortex.ai, VCOMMISSION, Walmart, Wise Online Money Transfer, WORDADS Affiliate Marketer. Also, check out Donna Kay KAKONGE Small Private School Owner/Teacher in the Pages Above and Donna Magazine Classes within the

Donna Magazine Store to Take a Choice of 62 Classes Via Zoom and Email for Ages 3 to 150, Formerly a Teacher with OUTSCHOOL and Retired College Professor

The store also has a Facebook Messenger system where you can receive instant help to your questions regarding the current 1,000 plus products in the Donna Magazine Store.

Let's take a closer look...

Amazon Prime

Amazon Prime

Check out this link for more information of the products available:

https://kakonged.wpcomstaging.com/product-category/amazon-prime/

Audible

Audible

Check out this link for more information on the products available:

https://kakonged.wpcomstaging.com/product-category/audible/

Banking and Business

Banking and Business

https://kakonged.wpcomstaging.com/product-category/banking/

Beauty and Health

Beauty and Health

https://kakonged.wpcomstaging.com/product-category/beauty-and-health/

Books

Books

https://kakonged.wpcomstaging.com/product-category/books/

Cars and Trucks

Cars and Trucks

https://kakonged.wpcomstaging.com/product-category/cars/

Clothing

Clothing

https://kakonged.wpcomstaging.com/product-category/clothing/

Dating

(Discretion Advised)

Dating

(Discretion Advised)

https://kakonged.wpcomstaging.com/product-category/dating/

Donna Magazine Classes

Donna Magazine Classes

https://kakonged.wpcomstaging.com/product-category/donna-magazine-classes/

Donna Magazine Etsy Store

(Free Gift with Purchase Offered)

Donna Magazine Etsy Store

(Free Gift with Purchase Offered)

https://kakonged.wpcomstaging.com/product-category/donna-magazine-beautifulturtles-etsy-store/

Food and Drink Items

Food and Drink Items

https://kakonged.wpcomstaging.com/product-category/food-items/

Fun Supplies

Fun Supplies

https://kakonged.wpcomstaging.com/product-category/recreational-supplies/

Furniture

Furniture

https://kakonged.wpcomstaging.com/product-category/furniture/

Gift Cards

Gift Cards

https://kakonged.wpcomstaging.com/product-category/gift-cards/

Gift Registries

Gift Registries

https://kakonged.wpcomstaging.com/product-category/gift-registries/

Hair

Hair

https://kakonged.wpcomstaging.com/product-category/hair/

Household Items

Household Items

https://kakonged.wpcomstaging.com/product-category/household-items/

Jobs

Jobs

https://kakonged.wpcomstaging.com/product-category/jobs/

Kindle

Kindle

https://kakonged.wpcomstaging.com/product-category/kindle/

Music

Music

https://kakonged.wpcomstaging.com/product-category/amazon-music/

Musical Instruments

Musical Instruments

https://kakonged.wpcomstaging.com/product-category/musical-instruments/

Online Legal Services

Online Legal Services

https://kakonged.wpcomstaging.com/product-category/online-law-united-kingdom/

Online School

Online School

https://kakonged.wpcomstaging.com/product-category/online-school/

Online Services

Online Services

https://kakonged.wpcomstaging.com/product-category/online-services/

Sale Items

Sale Items

https://kakonged.wpcomstaging.com/product-category/sale-items/

School Supplies

School Supplies

https://kakonged.wpcomstaging.
com/product-category/school-
supplies/

Shoes

Shoes

https://kakonged.wpcomstaging.com/product-category/shoes/

Sports Items

Sports Items

https://kakonged.wpcomstaging.com/product-category/sports-items/

Technology

Technology

https://kakonged.wpcomstaging.com/product-category/technology/

Tobacco – Using Addictions in a Positive Way

(Discretion Advised)

Tobacco – Using Addictions in a Positive Way

(Discretion is Advised)

https://kakonged.wpcomstaging.com/product-category/tobacco-using-addictions-in-positive-ways/

Toys

Toys

https://kakonged.wpcomstaging.com/product-category/toys/

Travel

Travel

https://kakonged.wpcomstaging.com/product-category/travel/

Watches/Jewelry

Watches/Jewelry

https://kakonged.wpcomstaging.com/product-category/watches-jewlery/

Conclusion

There will be a growing inventory to the Donna Magazine Store, plus additional affiliates.

Thank you in advance for shopping at the Donna Magazine Store. You will find many of your known and popular brands in the store.

About the Author

Multiple award-winning author/teacher/journalist/online lawyer/retired college professor/videographer/podcaster with over **30** years of writing expertise. Produced **15** daily articles for the *Toronto Star* and Young People's Press. **Six** stories hourly for the Canadian Broadcasting Corporation (CBC) for the radio and television news. There are three current daily affairs radio stories **5** days a week in English and French for Radio Canada International (RCI). Owner of Donna Magazine since October 1, 2007. The magazine has more than **10,900** multi-media articles and an audience of more than a billion people. The magazine is based on paid Donna Magazine Membership Inclusion. More than **42** years of experience teaching multi-platform writing at the college level worldwide, plus journalism, legal, and communications experience. Author, editor, the ghostwriter of more than **290** books, mainly self-published. Expertise in audio and video editing with industry-standard software. Expert editor with Grammarly Premium possession. With **155,217** books sold so far—six books in the Toronto Public Library and **29** other libraries throughout North America. With **92** of her titles in the online library, BIBLIOBOARD connected with the Toronto Public Library. Highest level of education a doctorate from the best university in Canada. Expert knowledge of both British and American written and spoken English. Undergraduate journalism degree, master's media studies degree, and doctorate education degree from the best schools in Canada. Law degree from a school in London, England. Teaching English as a Second Language certificate from an American school. Digital Humanities certificate from the non-profit unit of Harvard University, best American school. Dr. Donna Kay Cindy Kakonge, BJ (Carleton University - Ottawa),

MA (Concordia University - Montréal), TESOL (LinguaEdge - Online, United States), LLB (University of London International Programmes), EdD (OISE | University of Toronto)